Optavia Diet (k

Lean and Green.   d
Boost your Metabolism.

Green Recipes America

Table of Contents

Chapter 1: How to start - From beginners to Pro

Optavia dieting is a practice aimed at reducing weight or maintaining one's current weight. It recommends eating processed food referred to as fuelings and homemade meals (lean and green meals). It is believed that sticking to the brand's product (fuelings) and supplementing it with meat, veggies, and fat entrée every day; will keep you full and adequately nourished. And there are no worries about losing muscles as you'll be eating a lot of protein and consuming few calories. And in this way, the individuals involved can lose about 12 pounds in just 12 weeks using the 5&1 optimal weight plan.

Put simply, the Optavia diet is a program that focuses on lower calories and the reduction of carbohydrate meals. Doing this effectively combines packed food called fuelings with homemade meals, thus encouraging loss of weight. The name "Optavia" should sound like a new drug or eye-wear brand, but it is a weight loss program that has become famous thanks to the internet. Google named Optavia one of the hottest diets of 2018 in its year-end report, and Cake Boss Star Buddy Valastro said he lost weight thanks to this program.

The diet is not a simple one: the program limits calories and advises its affiliates to buy "supplies" to lose weight.

Optavia is a weight loss or maintenance program that recommends eating a mix of processed foods - called "supplies" - and homemade "lean green" meals.

The plan also recommends doing about 30 minutes of moderate-intensity exercise a day.

Medifast's team has released a new product line under the OPTAVIA brand, with the same macronutrients as its original Medifast products. The company claims that by working with its coaches and following a diet that includes OPTAVIA products, "a permanent transformation" is achieved.

In detail, keep the brand products called "Fuelings" and supplement them with an appetizer of meat, vegetables, and healthy fats every day; you will be full and well-fed. Plus, you won't lose muscle because you'll be eating many protein, fiber, and critical nutrients while consuming very few calories - about 800 to 1,000 for adults.

Customers lose around 12 pounds in 12 weeks with the Optimal Weight 5 & 1 plan.

Optavia adds a social support component access to a health coach who can answer questions and give encouragement.

How Does The Optavia Diet Work?

Most people follow the 5 & 1 program that incorporates five refills per day. With this program, customers eat 5 of Optavia's "supplies" and one lean and green low-calorie homemade meal per day.

You can also choose more than 60 options, including smoothies, bars, soups, cookies, and pudding, including high-quality protein and one probiotic that the brand claims to aid digestive health. Your sixth daily meal (that you can eat at any time) is built around cooked lean protein, three servings of non-starchy vegetables, and healthy fats.

During the diet, you will work with Optavia trainers and join a community to share your success. Once you've reached your weight goal, transitioning from the plan should be more comfortable as healthier ones replace your old habits. Optavia offers a specific product line through its 3 and 3 plans for weight maintenance.

For people who want a more flexible and high-calorie diet, OPTAVIA suggests the 4 & 2 & 1 plan that incorporates four meals, two lean and green meals, and one healthy snack, like a baked potato serving fruit.

Optavia also sells specific programs for people with diabetes, nursing moms, the elderly and teenagers.

Benefits of Optavia Diet

1. Packaged products offer convenience

Optavia's smoothies, soups, and other meal replacement products are shipped to your door, providing a level of convenience that many other diets don't offer.

Even if you will need to purchase your ingredients for "lean and green" meals, Optavia's home delivery option for "supplies" helps a lot.

Once the products arrive, they are easy to prepare and make great takeaway meals.

2. Achieve rapid weight loss

Most healthy people need around 1,600-3,000 calories per day to maintain their weight. Limiting that amount to a minimum of 800 guarantees weight loss for most people.

Optavia's 5 & 1 plan is designed for rapid weight loss, making it a viable option for someone with a medical reason to lose weight fast.

3. Eliminate the guesswork

Some people say that the most challenging part of a diet is the mental effort to figure out what to eat each day or at each meal.

Optavia relieves the stress of meal planning and "decision fatigue" by offering users approved foods with "supplies" and guidelines for "lean and green" meals.

4. Offers social support

Social support is an essential component of the success of any weight loss program. Optavia's coaching program and group call ensure integrated encouragement and support for users.

Pesto Zucchini Noodles

Time: 30 minutes

Serve: 4

Ingredients:

- 4 zucchini, spiralized

- 1 tbsp avocado oil

- 2 garlic cloves, chopped

- 2/3 cup olive oil

- 1/3 cup parmesan cheese, grated

- 2 cups fresh basil

- 1/3 cup almonds

- 1/8 tsp black pepper

- ¾ tsp sea salt

Directions:

1. Add zucchini noodles into a colander and sprinkle with ¼ teaspoon of salt. Cover and let sit for 30 minutes. Drain zucchini noodles well and pat dry.

2. Preheat the oven to 400 F.

3. Place almonds on a parchment-lined baking sheet and bake for 6-8 minutes.

Transfer toasted almonds into the food processor and process until coarse.

4. Add olive oil, cheese, basil, garlic, pepper, and remaining salt in a food processor with almonds and process until pesto texture.

5. Heat avocado oil in a large pan over medium-high heat.

6. Add zucchini noodles and cook for 4-5 minutes.

7. Pour pesto over zucchini noodles, mix well and cook for 1 minute.

8. Serve immediately with baked salmon.

Nutritional Value (Amount per Serving):

Calories 525 Fat 47.4 g Carbs 9.3 g Sugar 3.8 g Protein 16.6 g Cholesterol 30 mg

Baked Cod & Vegetables

Time: 30 minutes

Serve: 4

Ingredients:

- 1 lb cod fillets

- 8 oz asparagus, chopped

- 3 cups broccoli, chopped

- ¼ cup parsley, minced

- ½ tsp lemon pepper seasoning

- ½ tsp paprika

- ¼ cup olive oil

- ¼ cup lemon juice

- 1 tsp salt

Directions:

Preheat the oven to 400 F. Cover the pan with baking paper and

1. Set aside.

2. In a small bowl, mix lemon juice, paprika, olive oil, lemon pepper seasoning, and salt.

3. Place fish fillets in the middle of the parchment paper. Place broccoli and asparagus around the fish fillets.

4. Pour lemon juice mixture over the fish fillets and top with parsley.

5. Bake in preheated oven for 13-15 minutes.

6. Serve and enjoy.

Nutritional Value (Amount per Serving):

Calories 240 Fat 14.1 g Carbs 7.6 g Sugar 2.6 g Protein 23.7 g Cholesterol 56 mg

Parmesan Zucchini

Time: 30 minutes

Serve: 4

Ingredients:

- 4 zucchini, quartered lengthwise

- 2 tbsp fresh parsley, chopped

- 2 tbsp olive oil

- ¼ tsp garlic powder

- ½ tsp dried basil

- ½ tsp dried oregano

- ½ tsp dried thyme

- ½ cup parmesan cheese, grated

- Pepper

- Salt

Directions:

Preheat the oven to 350 F. Line baking sheet with parchment paper and set aside.

1. In a small bowl, mix parmesan cheese, garlic powder, basil, oregano, thyme, pepper, and salt.

17

2. Arrange zucchini onto the prepared baking sheet and drizzle with oil and sprinkle with parmesan cheese mixture.

3. Bake in preheated oven for 15 minutes, then broil for 2 minutes or until lightly golden brown.

4. Garnish with parsley and serve immediately.

Nutritional Value (Amount per Serving):

Calories 244 Fat 16.4 g Carbs 7 g Sugar 3.5 g Protein 14.5 g Cholesterol 30 mg

Chicken Zucchini Noodles

Time: 25 minutes

Serve: 2

Ingredients:

- 1 large zucchini, spiralized

- 1 chicken breast, skinless & boneless

- ½ tbsp jalapeno, minced

- 2 garlic cloves, minced

- ½ tsp ginger, minced

- ½ tbsp fish sauce

- 2 tbsp coconut cream

- ½ tbsp honey

- ½ lime juice

- 1 tbsp peanut butter

- 1 carrot, chopped

- 2 tbsp cashews, chopped

- ¼ cup fresh cilantro, chopped

- 1 tbsp olive oil

- Pepper

- Salt

Directions:

Heat the olive oil in a pan.

1. Season chicken breast with pepper and salt. Once the oil is hot, add chicken breast into the pan and cook for 3-4 minutes per side or until cooked.

2. Remove chicken breast from pan. Shred chicken breast with a fork and set aside.

3. In a small bowl, mix peanut butter, jalapeno, garlic, ginger, fish sauce, coconut cream, honey, and lime juice. Set aside.

4. In a large mixing bowl, combine spiralized zucchini, carrots, cashews, cilantro, and shredded chicken.

5. Pour peanut butter mixture over zucchini noodles and toss to combine.

6. Serve immediately and enjoy.

Nutritional Value (Amount per Serving):

Calories 353 Fat 21.1 g Carbs 20.5 g Sugar 10.8 g Protein 24.5 g Cholesterol 54 mg

Tomato Cucumber Avocado Salad

Time: 15 minutes

Serve: 4

Ingredients:

- 12 oz cherry tomatoes, cut in half

- 5 small cucumbers, chopped

- 3 small avocados, chopped

- ½ tsp ground black pepper

- 2 tbsp olive oil

- 2 tbsp fresh lemon juice

- ¼ cup fresh cilantro, chopped

- 1 tsp sea salt

Directions:

1. Add cherry tomatoes, cucumbers, avocados, and cilantro into the large mixing bowl and mix well.

2. Mix olive oil, lemon juice, black pepper, and salt and pour over salad.

3. Toss well and serve immediately.

Nutritional Value (Amount per Serving):

Calories 442 Fat 37.1 g Carbs 30.3 g Sugar 9.4 g Protein 6.2 g
Cholesterol 0 mg

Creamy Cauliflower Soup

Time: 30 minutes

Serve: 6

Ingredients:

- 5 cups cauliflower rice

- 8 oz cheddar cheese, grated

- 2 cups unsweetened almond milk

- 2 cups vegetable stock

- 2 tbsp water

- 1 small onion, chopped

- 2 garlic cloves, minced

- 1 tbsp olive oil

- Pepper

- Salt

Directions:

1. Heat olive oil in a large stockpot over medium heat.

2. Add onion and garlic and cook for 1-2 minutes.

3. Add cauliflower rice and water. Cover and cook for 5-7 minutes.

4. Now add vegetable stock and almond milk and stir well. Bring to boil.

5. Turn heat to low and simmer for 5 minutes.

6. Turn off the heat. Slowly add cheddar cheese and stir until smooth.

7. Season soup with pepper and salt.

8. Stir well and serve hot.

Nutritional Value (Amount per Serving):

Calories 214 Fat 16.5 g Carbs 7.3 g Sugar 3 g Protein 11.6 g Cholesterol 40 mg

Taco Zucchini Boats

Time: 70 minutes

Serve: 4

Ingredients:

- 4 medium zucchinis, cut in half lengthwise

- ¼ cup fresh cilantro, chopped

- ½ cup cheddar cheese, shredded

- ¼ cup of water

- 4 oz tomato sauce

- 2 tbsp bell pepper, mined

- ½ small onion, minced

- ½ tsp oregano

- 1 tsp paprika

- 1 tsp chili powder

- 1 tsp cumin

- 1 tsp garlic powder

- 1 lb lean ground turkey

- ½ cup of salsa

- 1 tsp kosher salt

Directions:

1. Preheat the oven to 400 F.

2. Add ¼ cup of salsa to the bottom of the baking dish.

3. Using a spoon, hollow out the center of the zucchini halves.

4. Chop the scooped-out flesh of zucchini and set aside ¾ of a cup of chopped flesh.

5. Add zucchini halves to the boiling water and cook for 1 minute. Remove zucchini halves from water.

6. Add ground turkey in a large pan and cook until meat is no longer pink. Add spices and mix well.

7. Add reserved zucchini flesh, water, tomato sauce, bell pepper, and onion. Stir well and cover, simmer over low heat for 20 minutes.

8. Stuff zucchini boats with taco meat and top each with one tablespoon of shredded cheddar cheese.

Place zucchini boats in a baking dish. Cover the dish with paper and bake in a preheated oven

1. 35 minutes.

2. Top with remaining salsa and chopped cilantro.

3. Serve and enjoy.

Nutritional Value (Amount per Serving):

Calories 297 Fat 13.7 g Carbs 17.2 g Sugar 9.3 g Protein 30.2 g Cholesterol 96 mg

Healthy Broccoli Salad

Time: 25 minutes

Serve: 6

Ingredients:

- 3 cups broccoli, chopped

- 1 tbsp apple cider vinegar

- ½ cup Greek yogurt

- 2 tbsp sunflower seeds

- 3 bacon slices, cooked and chopped

- 1/3 cup onion, sliced

- ¼ tsp stevia

Directions:

1. In a mixing bowl, mix broccoli, onion, and bacon.

2. In a small bowl, mix yogurt, vinegar, and stevia and pour over broccoli mixture. Stir to combine.

3. Sprinkle sunflower seeds on top of the salad.

4. Store salad in the refrigerator for 30 minutes.

5. Serve and enjoy.

Nutritional Value (Amount per Serving):

Calories 90 Fat 4.9 g Carbs 5.4 g Sugar 2.5 g Protein 6.2 g
Cholesterol 12 mg

Delicious Zucchini Quiche

Time: 60 minutes

Serve: 8

Ingredients:

- 6 eggs

- 2 medium zucchini, shredded

- ½ tsp dried basil

- 2 garlic cloves, minced

- 1 tbsp dry onion, minced

- 2 tbsp parmesan cheese, grated

- 2 tbsp fresh parsley, chopped

- ½ cup olive oil

- 1 cup cheddar cheese, shredded

- ¼ cup coconut flour

- ¾ cup almond flour

- ½ tsp salt

Directions:

1. Preheat the oven to 350 F. Grease a 9-inch pie dish and set aside.

2. Squeeze out excess liquid from zucchini.

3. Add all ingredients into the large bowl and mix until well combined. Pour into the prepared pie dish.

4. Bake in preheated oven for 45-60 minutes or until set.

5. Remove from the oven and let it cool completely.

6. Slice and serve.

Nutritional Value (Amount per Serving):

Calories 288 Fat 26.3 g Carbs 5 g Sugar 1.6 g Protein 11 g Cholesterol 139 mg

Turkey Spinach Egg Muffins

Time: 30 minutes

Serve: 3

Ingredients:

- 5 egg whites

- 2 eggs

- ¼ cup cheddar cheese, shredded

- ¼ cup spinach, chopped

- ¼ cup milk

- 3 lean breakfast turkey sausage

- Pepper

- Salt

Directions:

1. Preheat the oven to 350 F. Grease muffin tray cups and set aside.

2. In a pan, brown the turkey sausage links over medium-high heat until the sausage is brown from all the sides.

3. Cut sausage into ½-inch pieces and set aside.

4. In a large bowl, whisk together eggs, egg whites, milk, pepper, and salt. Stir in spinach.

5. Pour egg mixture into the prepared muffin tray.

6. Divide sausage and cheese evenly between each muffin cup.

7. Bake in a preheated oven for 20 minutes or until muffins are set.

8. Serve warm and enjoy.

Nutritional Value (Amount per Serving):

Calories 123 Fat 6.8 g Carbs 1.9 g Sugar 1.6 g Protein 13.3 g Cholesterol 123 mg

Chicken Casserole

Time: 40 minutes

Serve: 4

Ingredients:

• 1 lb cooked chicken, shredded

• ¼ cup Greek yogurt

• 1 cup cheddar cheese, shredded

• ½ cup of salsa

• 4 oz cream cheese, softened

• 4 cups cauliflower florets

• 1/8 tsp black pepper

• ½ tsp kosher salt

Directions:

1. Add cauliflower florets into the microwave-safe dish and cook for 10 minutes or until tender.

2. Add cream cheese and microwave for 30 seconds more. Stir well.

3. Add chicken, yogurt, cheddar cheese, salsa, pepper, and salt, and stir everything well.

4. Preheat the oven to 375 F.

5. Bake in preheated oven for 20 minutes.

6. Serve hot and enjoy.

7. **Nutritional Value (Amount per Serving):**

Calories 429 Fat 23 g Carbs 9.6 g Sugar 4.7 g Protein 45.4 g Cholesterol 149 mg

Shrimp Cucumber Salad

Time: 20 minutes

Serve: 4

Ingredients:

- 1 lb shrimp, cooked

- 1 bell pepper, sliced

- 2 green onions, sliced

- ½ cup fresh cilantro, chopped

- 2 cucumbers, sliced

- For dressing:

- 2 tbsp fresh mint leaves, chopped

- 1 tsp sesame seeds

- ½ tsp red pepper flakes

- 1 tbsp olive oil

- ¼ cup rice wine vinegar

- ¼ cup lime juice

- 1 Serrano chili pepper, minced

- 3 garlic cloves, minced

- ½ tsp salt

Directions:

1. In a small bowl, whisk together all dressing ingredients and set aside.

2. In a mixing bowl, mix shrimp, bell pepper, green onion, cilantro, and cucumbers.

3. Pour dressing over salad and toss well.

4. Serve and enjoy.

Nutritional Value (Amount per Serving):

Calories 219 Fat 6.1 g Carbs 11.3 g Sugar 4.2 g Protein 27.7 g Cholesterol 239 mg

Asparagus & Shrimp Stir Fry
Time: 20 minutes

Serve: 4

Ingredients:

- 1 lb asparagus

- 1 lb shrimp

- 2 tbsp lemon juice

- 1 tbsp soy sauce

- 1 tsp ginger, minced

- 1 garlic clove, minced

- 1 tsp red pepper flakes

- ¼ cup olive oil

- Pepper

- Salt

Directions:

1. Heat 2 tablespoons of oil in a large pan over medium-high heat.

2. Add shrimp to the pan and season with red pepper flakes, pepper, salt, and cook for 5 minutes.

3. Remove shrimp from pan and set aside.

4. Add remaining oil in the same pan. Add garlic, ginger, and asparagus, stir frequently, and cook until asparagus is tender about 5 minutes.

5. Return shrimp to the pan. Add lemon juice and soy sauce and stir until well combined.

6. Serve hot and enjoy.

Nutritional Value (Amount per Serving):

Calories 274 Fat 14.8 g Carbs 7.4 g Sugar 2.4 g Protein 28.8 g Cholesterol 239 mg

Turkey Burgers

Time: 30 minutes

Serve: 4

Ingredients:

- 1 lb lean ground turkey

- 2 green onions, sliced

- ¼ cup basil leaves, shredded

- 2 garlic cloves, minced

- 2 medium zucchini, shredded and squeeze out all the liquid

- ½ tsp black pepper

- ½ tsp sea salt

Directions:

1. Heat grill to medium heat.
2. Add all ingredients to the bowl and mix until well blended.
3. Make four equal shapes of patties from the mixture.
4. Spray one piece of foil with cooking spray.
5. Place prepared patties on the foil and grill for 10 minutes. Turn patties to the other side and grill for 10 minutes more.
6. Serve and enjoy.

Nutritional Value (Amount per Serving):

Calories 183 Fat 8.3 g Carbs 4.5 g Sugar 1.9 g Protein 23.8 g Cholesterol 81 mg

Broccoli Kale Salmon Burgers

Time: 30 minutes

Serve: 5

Ingredients:

- 2 eggs

- ½ cup onion, chopped

- ½ cup broccoli, chopped

- ½ cup kale, chopped

- ½ tsp garlic powder

- 2 tbsp lemon juice

- ½ cup almond flour

- 15 oz can salmon, drained and bones removed

- ½ tsp salt

Directions:

1. Line one plate with parchment paper and set aside.

2. Add all ingredients into the large bowl and mix until well combined.

3. Make five equal shapes of patties from the mixture and place them on a prepared plate.

4. Place plate in the refrigerator for 30 minutes.

5. Spray a large pan with cooking spray and heat over medium heat.

6. Once the pan is hot, then add patties and cook for 5-7 minutes per side.

7. Serve and enjoy.

Nutritional Value (Amount per Serving):

Calories 221 Fat 12.6 g Carbs 5.2 g Sugar 1.4 g Protein 22.1 g Cholesterol 112 mg

Pan Seared Cod

Time: 25 minutes

Serve: 4

Ingredients:

- 1 ¾ lbs cod fillets

- 1 tbsp ranch seasoning

- 4 tsp olive oil

Directions:

1. Heat oil in a large pan over medium-high heat.

2. Season fish fillets with ranch seasoning.

3. Once the oil is hot, then place fish fillets in a pan and cook for 6-8 minutes on each side.

4. Serve immediately and enjoy.

Nutritional Value (Amount per Serving):

Calories 207 Fat 6.4 g Carbs 0 g Sugar 0 g Protein 35.4 g Cholesterol 97 mg

Quick Lemon Pepper Salmon
Time: 18 minutes

Serve: 4

Ingredients:

- 1 ½ lbs salmon fillets

- ½ tsp ground black pepper

- 1 tsp dried oregano

- 2 garlic cloves, minced

- ¼ cup olive oil

- 1 lemon juice

- 1 tsp sea salt

Directions:

1. In a large bowl, mix lemon juice, olive oil, garlic, oregano, black pepper, and salt.

2. Add fish fillets in the bowl and coat well with the marinade, and place in the refrigerator for 15 minutes.

3. Preheat the grill.

4. Brush grill grates with oil.

5. Place marinated salmon fillets on hot grill and cook for 4 minutes, then turn salmon fillets to the other side and cook for 4 minutes more.

6. Serve and enjoy.

Nutritional Value (Amount per Serving):

Calories 340 Fat 23.3 g Carbs 1.2 g Sugar 0.3 g Protein 33.3 g Cholesterol 75 mg

Healthy Salmon Salad

Time: 20 minutes

Serve: 2

Ingredients:

- 2 salmon fillets
- 2 tbsp olive oil
- ¼ cup onion, chopped
- 1 cucumber, peeled and sliced
- 1 avocado, diced
- 2 tomatoes, chopped
- 4 cups baby spinach
- Pepper
- Salt

Directions:

1. Heat the olive oil in a pan.
2. Season salmon fillets with pepper and salt. Place fish fillets in a pan and cook for 4-5 minutes.
3. Turn fish fillets and cook for 2-3 minutes more.
4. Divide remaining ingredients evenly between two bowls, then top with cooked fish fillet.
5. Serve and enjoy.

Nutritional Value (Amount per Serving):

Calories 350 Fat 23.2 g Carbs 15.3 g Sugar 6.6 g Protein 25 g
Cholesterol 18 mg

Pan Seared Tilapia

Time: 18 minutes

Serve: 2

Ingredients:

- 18 oz tilapia fillets

- ¼ tsp lemon pepper

- ½ tsp parsley flakes

- ¼ tsp garlic powder

- 1 tsp Cajun seasoning

- ½ tsp dried oregano

- 2 tbsp olive oil

Directions:

1. Heat the olive oil in a pan.
2. Season fish fillets with lemon pepper, parsley flakes, garlic powder, Cajun seasoning, and oregano.
3. Place fish fillets in the pan and cook for 3-4 minutes on each side.
4. Serve and enjoy.

Nutritional Value (Amount per Serving):

Calories 333 Fat 16.4 g Carbs 0.7 g Sugar 0.1 g Protein 47.6 g Cholesterol 124 mg

53

Chicken Cauliflower Rice

Time: 25 minutes

Serve: 4

Ingredients:

- 1 cauliflower head, chopped

- 2 cups cooked chicken, shredded

- 1 tsp olive oil

- 1 tsp garlic powder

- 1 tsp chili powder

- 1 tsp cumin

- 1/4 cup tomatoes, diced

- Salt

Directions:

1. Add cauliflower into the food processor and process until you get rice size pieces.

2. Heat oil in a pan over high heat.

3. Add cauliflower rice and chicken in a pan and cook for 5-7 minutes.

4. Add garlic powder, chili powder, cumin, tomatoes, and salt. Stir well and cook for 7-10 minutes more.

5. Serve and enjoy.

Nutritional Value (Amount per Serving):

Calories 140 Fat 3.6 g Carbs 5 g Sugar 2 g Protein 22 g Cholesterol 54 mg

Easy Spinach Muffins

Time: 25 minutes

Serve: 12

Ingredients:

- 10 eggs

- 2 cups spinach, chopped

- 1/4 tsp garlic powder

- 1/4 tsp onion powder

- 1/2 tsp dried basil

- 1 1/2 cups parmesan cheese, grated

- Salt

Directions:

Preheat the oven to 400 F. Grease muffin tin and set aside.

1. In a large bowl, whisk eggs with basil, garlic powder, onion powder, and salt.

2. Add cheese and spinach and stir well.

3. Pour egg mixture into the prepared muffin tin and bake 15 minutes.

4. Serve and enjoy.

Nutritional Value (Amount per Serving):

Calories 110 Fat 7 g Carbs 1 g Sugar 0.3 g Protein 9 g Cholesterol 165 mg

Healthy Cauliflower Grits

Time: 2 hours 10 minutes

Serve: 8

Ingredients:

- 6 cups cauliflower rice

- 1/4 tsp garlic powder

- 1 cup cream cheese

- 1/2 cup vegetable stock

- 1/4 tsp onion powder

- 1/2 tsp pepper

- 1 tsp salt

Directions:

1. Add all ingredients into the slow cooker and stir well combine.

2. Cover and cook on low for 2 hours.

3. Stir and serve.

Nutritional Value (Amount per Serving):

Calories 126 Fat 10 g Carbs 5 g Sugar 2 g Protein 4 g Cholesterol 31 mg

Optavia Cloud Bread

Preparation Time: 30 minutes

Cooking Time: 30 minutes

Servings: 1

INGREDIENTS:

1/4 cup fat-free 0%

Plain Greek yogurt (4.4 oz)

1 egg, separated

1/32 teaspoon cream of tartar

1/2 packet sweetener (a granulated sweetener just like stevia)

DIRECTIONS:

1. For about 30 minutes before making this meal, place the Kitchen Aid Bowl and the freezer's whisk attachment.

2. Preheat your oven to 30 degrees.

3. Eliminate the bowl and whisk attachment from the freezer.

4. Separate the eggs. Now put the egg whites in the Kitchen Aid Bowl, and they should be in a different medium-sized bowl.

5. In the medium-sized bowl containing the yolks, mix in the sweetener and yogurt.

6. In the bowl containing the egg white, add in the cream of tartar. Beat this mixture until the egg whites turn to stiff peaks.

7. Now, take the egg yolk mixture and carefully fold it into the egg whites. Be cautious and avoid over-stirring.

8. On a parchment paper, place it on a baking tray and spray with cooking spray.

9. Scoop out six equally sized "blobs" of the "dough" onto the parchment paper.

10. Bake for about 25–35 minutes (make sure you check when it is 25 minutes, in some ovens, they are done at this timestamp). You will know they are done as they will get brownish at the top and have some crack.

11. Most people like them cold against being warm.

12. Most people like to re-heat in a toast oven or toaster to get them a little bit crispy.

NUTRITION:

Calories: 0

Protein: 0g

Carbohydrates: 0g

Fats: 0g

Rosemary Cauliflower Rolls

Preparation Time: 15 minutes

Cooking Time: 30 minutes

Servings: 1 (3 biscuits per serving)

INGREDIENTS:

1/12 cup almond flour

1 cup grated cauliflower

1/12 cup reduced-fat, shredded mozzarella or cheddar cheese

1/2 eggs

1/2 tablespoons fresh rosemary, finely chopped

½ teaspoon salt

DIRECTIONS:

1. Preheat your oven to 4000F.

2. Pour all the ingredients into a medium-sized bowl.

3. Scoop cauliflower mixture into 12 evenly sized rolls/biscuits onto a lightly greased and foil-lined baking sheet.

4. Bake until it turns golden brown, which should be achieved in about 30 minutes.

5. Note: if you want to have the outside of the rolls/biscuits crisp, then broil for some minutes before serving.

NUTRITION:

Calories: 138

Protein: 11g

Carbohydrates: 8g

Fats: 7g

Tomato Braised Cauliflower with Chicken

Preparation Time: 15 minutes

Cooking Time: 30 minutes

Servings: 1

INGREDIENTS:

1 garlic clove, sliced

3/4 scallions, to be trimmed and cut into 1-inch pieces 1/8 teaspoon dried oregano

1/8 teaspoon red pepper flakes

1/4 cups cauliflower

3/4 cups diced canned tomatoes

1/4 cup fresh basil, gently torn

1/8 teaspoon each of pepper and salt, divided

3/4 teaspoon olive oil

3/4 pound boneless, skinless chicken breasts

DIRECTIONS:

1. Get a saucepan and combine the garlic, scallions, oregano, crushed red pepper, cauliflower, tomato, and add ¼ cup of water. Get everything boil together, add ¼ teaspoon of pepper and salt for seasoning, and then cover the pot with a lid. Let it simmer for 10 minutes and stir as often as possible until you observe that the cauliflower is tender. Now, wrap up the seasoning with the remaining ¼ teaspoon of pepper and salt.

2. Using olive oil, toss the chicken breast and let it roast in the oven with the heat of 4500F for 20 minutes and an internal temperature of 1650F. Allow the chicken to rest for like 10 minutes.

3. Now slice the chicken and serve on a bed of tomato-braised cauliflower.

NUTRITION:

Calories: 290

Fats: 10g

Carbohydrates: 13g

Protein: 38g

Cheeseburger Soup

Preparation Time: 15 minutes

Cooking Time: 30 minutes

Servings: 1

INGREDIENTS:

1/16 cup chopped onion

1 quantity of (14.5 oz) can dice a tomato

1/4 pound 90% lean ground beef

3/16 cup chopped celery

1/4 teaspoons Worcestershire sauce

1/2 cup chicken broth

1/8 teaspoon salt

1/4 teaspoon dried parsley

2/3 cups of baby spinach

1/8 teaspoon ground pepper

1 oz. reduced-fat shredded cheddar cheese

DIRECTIONS:

1. Get a large soup pot and cook the beef until it becomes brown. Add the celery, onion, and sauté until it becomes tender. Make sure to drain the excess liquid.

2. Stir in the broth, tomatoes, parsley, Worcestershire sauce, pepper, and salt. Cover and wait for it to simmer on low heat for about 20 minutes.

3. Add spinach and leave it to cook until it becomes wilted in about 1–3 minutes. Top each of your servings with 1 oz of cheese.

NUTRITION:

Calories: 400

Carbohydrates: 11g

Protein: 44g

Fats: 20g

Braised Collard Beans in Peanut Sauce with Pork Tenderloin

Preparation Time: 25 minutes

Cooking Time: 35 minutes

Servings: 1

INGREDIENTS:

1/2 cups chicken stock

3 cups chopped collard greens

1 1/2 tablespoons powdered peanut butter

3/4 cloves of garlic, crushed

1/4 teaspoon salt

1/8 teaspoon allspice

1/8 teaspoon black pepper

1/2 teaspoons lemon juice

3/8 teaspoon hot sauce

1/8 pound pork tenderloin

DIRECTIONS:

1. Get a pot with a tight-fitting lid and combine the collards with the garlic, chicken stock, hot sauce, and half of the pepper and salt. Cook on low heat for about 1 hour or until the collards become tender.

2. Once the collards are tender, stir in the allspice, lemon juice. And they have powdered peanut butter. Keep warm.

3. Season the pork tenderloin with the remaining pepper and salt, and broil in a toaster oven for 10 minutes when you have an internal temperature of 1450F. Make sure to turn the tenderloin every 2 minutes to achieve an even browning all over. After that, you can take away the pork from the oven and allow it to rest for like 5 minutes.

4. Slice the pork as you will like and serve it on top of the braised greens.

NUTRITION:

Calories: 320

Fats: 10g

Carbohydrates: 15g

Protein: 45g

Zucchini Pizza Casserole

Preparation Time: 15 minutes

Cooking Time: 50–60 minutes

Servings: 1

INGREDIENTS:

¼ teaspoon salt

¼ cup grated parmesan cheese

1/2 eggs

2/3 cups shredded unpeeled zucchini (this is about two medium zucchinis)

1 oz. reduced-fat, shredded cheddar cheese, divided

1 oz. reduced-fat, shredded mozzarella cheese, divided 1/8 pound 90–94% of lean ground beef

Cooking spray

1 quantity 14.5 oz. can petite diced Italian tomatoes

1/8 cup chopped onion

1/2 small green bell pepper, chopped

DIRECTIONS:

1. Preheat your oven to over 4000F.

2. Place zucchini in a strainer and sprinkle it with salt. Let it stand for about 10 minutes, and after that, press it to drain its moisture.

3. Combine zucchini with eggs, parmesan, and half of cheddar cheese and mozzarella.

4. Press the mixture into a lightly greased baking dish and bake while uncovered for about 20 minutes.

5. Cook the onion and beef in a medium skillet until it becomes done. Drain any leftover liquid, and then stir in the tomatoes.

6. Pour the beef mixture over the zucchini and sprinkle with the remaining mozzarella cheese and cheddar. Top with green pepper

7. Bake for an extra 20 minutes or until it becomes heated all through.

NUTRITION:

Calories: 478

Protein: 30g

Carbohydrates: 22g

Fats: 29g

Tofu Power Bowl

Preparation Time: 10 minutes

Cooking Time: 15–20 minutes

Servings: 1

INGREDIENTS:

15 oz. extra-firm tofu

1 teaspoon rice vinegar

2 tablespoons soy sauce

1 teaspoon sesame oil

½ cup grated cauliflower

½ cup grated eggplant

½ cup chopped kale

DIRECTIONS:

1. Press tofu. Place tofu strips in multiple layers of paper towel or a clean dishcloth on top of a cutting board or plate. Place another clean dish towel or paper towels on top of the tofu. Place a weight on top of this second layer (this can be a large plate with canned foods on top or hardcover books, or a stack of leaves). Let it sit for not less than 15 minutes, and then cut the tofu into 1-inch cubes.

2. Combine both the vinegar and soy sauce in a small bowl and whisk together.

3. Get a large skillet and heat the sesame oil in it. Place cubed tofu to cover one half of the skillet, and the cubed eggplant should cover the other half. Cook both together until they become slightly brown and tender in about 10–12 minutes. Remove from skillet and keep aside. Now, add kale and sauté until they become wilted in about 3–5 minutes.

4. Microwave the already grated cauliflower in a small bowl with one teaspoon of water for about 3–4 minutes until it becomes tender.

5. Arrange the cauliflower "rice" with tofu, eggplant, and kale in a bowl.

NUTRITION:

Calories: 117

Protein: 14g

Carbohydrates: 2.2g

Fats: 7g

Grilled Veggie Kabobs

Preparation Time: 15 minutes

Cooking Time: 12 to 15 minute

Servings: 1

INGREDIENTS:

Marinade:

½ cup balsamic vinegar

1/3 tablespoons minced thyme

1/4 tablespoons minced rosemary

1/2 cloves garlic, peeled and minced

Sea salt, to taste (optional)

Freshly ground black pepper, to taste

Veggies:

1/3 cups cherry tomatoes

1/3 red bell pepper, it should be seeded and cut into 1-inch pieces 1/3 green bell pepper, without seeds and cut into 1-inch pieces 1/3 medium yellow squash, cut into 1-inch rounds

1/3 medium zucchini, cut into 1-inch rounds

1/3 medium red onion skinned and cut into large chunks

Special Equipment:

Two bamboo skewers, make sure to soak it in water for 30 minutes.

DIRECTIONS:

1. Preheat the grill to medium heat.

2. In making the marinade: In a small bowl, stir together the balsamic vinegar, thyme, rosemary, garlic, salt (if desired), and pepper.

3. Thread veggies onto skewers, alternating between different-colored veggies.

4. Grill the veggies for 12 to 15 minutes until softened, and lightly it was charred, brushing the veggies with the marinade and flipping the skewers every 4 to 5 minutes.

5. Remove from the grill and serve hot.

NUTRITION:

Calories: 98

Fat: 0.7g

Carbs: 19.2g

Protein: 3.8g

Fiber: 3.4g

Grilled Cauliflower Steaks

Preparation Time: 10 minutes

Cooking Time: 57 minutes

Servings: 1

INGREDIENTS:

1/2 medium heads cauliflower

1/2 medium shallots, peeled and minced Water, as needed

1/2 clove garlic, peeled and minced

½ teaspoon ground fennel

½ teaspoon minced sage

Spinach Tomato Frittata

Time: 30 minutes

Serve: 8

Ingredients:

- 12 eggs

- 2 cups baby spinach, shredded

- 1/4 cup sun-dried tomatoes, sliced

- 1/2 tsp dried basil

- 1/4 cup parmesan cheese, grated

- Pepper

- Salt

Directions:

1. Preheat the oven to 425 F. Grease oven-safe pan and set aside.

2. In a large bowl, whisk eggs with pepper and salt. Add remaining ingredients and stir to combine.

3. Pour egg mixture into the prepared pan and bake for 20 minutes.

4. Slice and serve.

Nutritional Value (Amount per Serving):

Calories 116 Fat 7 g Carbs 1 g Sugar 1 g Protein 10 g Cholesterol 250 mg

Tofu Scramble

Time: 17 minutes

Serve: 2

Ingredients:

- 1/2 block firm tofu, crumbled

- 1 cup spinach

- 1/4 cup zucchini, chopped

- 1 tbsp olive oil

- 1 tomato, chopped

- 1/4 tsp ground cumin

- 1 tbsp turmeric

- 1 tbsp coriander, chopped

- 1 tbsp chives, chopped

- Pepper

- Salt

Directions:

1. Heat the oil in a pan.
2. Add tomato, zucchini, and spinach and sauté for 2 minutes.
3. Add tofu, turmeric, cumin, pepper, and salt, and sauté for 5 minutes.
4. Garnish with chives and coriander.
5. Serve and enjoy.

Nutritional Value (Amount per Serving):

Calories 102 Fat 8 g Carbs 5 g Sugar 2 g Protein 3 g Cholesterol 0 mg

Shrimp & Zucchini

Time: 30 minutes

Serve: 4

Ingredients:

- 1 lb shrimp, peeled and deveined

- 1 zucchini, chopped

- 1 summer squash, chopped

- 2 tbsp olive oil

- 1/2 small onion, chopped

- 1/2 tsp paprika

- 1/2 tsp garlic powder

- 1/2 tsp onion powder

- Pepper

- Salt

Directions:

1. In a bowl, mix paprika, garlic powder, onion powder, pepper, and salt. Add shrimp and toss well.

2. Heat 1 tablespoon of oil in a pan over medium heat,

3. Add shrimp and cook for 2 minutes on each side or until shrimp turns pink.

4. Transfer shrimp on a plate.

5. Add remaining oil to a pan.

6. Add onion, summer squash, and zucchini, and cook for 6-8 minutes or until vegetables are softened.

7. Return shrimp to the pan and cook for 1 minute.

8. Serve and enjoy.

Nutritional Value (Amount per Serving):

Calories 215 Fat 9 g Carbs 6 g Sugar 2 g Protein 27 g Cholesterol 239 mg

Baked Dijon Salmon

Time: 30 minutes

Serve: 5

Ingredients:

- 1 1/2 lbs salmon

- 1/4 cup Dijon mustard

- 1/4 cup fresh parsley, chopped

- 1 tbsp garlic, chopped

- 1 tbsp olive oil

- 1 tbsp fresh lemon juice

- Pepper

- Salt

Directions:

1. Preheat the oven to 375 F. Line baking sheet with parchment paper.

2. Arrange salmon fillets on a prepared baking sheet.

3. In a small bowl, mix garlic, oil, lemon juice, Dijon mustard, parsley, pepper, and salt.

4. Brush salmon top with garlic mixture.

5. Bake for 18-20 minutes.

6. Serve and enjoy.

Nutritional Value (Amount per Serving):

Calories 217 Fat 11 g Carbs 2 g Sugar 0.2 g Protein 27 g Cholesterol 60 mg

Cauliflower Spinach Rice

Time: 15 minutes

Serve: 4

Ingredients:

- 5 oz baby spinach

- 4 cups cauliflower rice

- 1 tsp garlic, minced

- 3 tbsp olive oil

- 1 fresh lime juice

- 1/4 cup vegetable broth

- 1/4 tsp chili powder

- Pepper

- Salt

Directions:

1. Heat the olive oil in a pan.
2. Add garlic and sauté for 30 seconds. Add cauliflower rice, chili powder, pepper, and salt and cook for 2 minutes.
3. Add broth and lime juice and stir well.
4. Add spinach and stir until spinach is wilted.
5. Serve and enjoy.

Nutritional Value (Amount per Serving):

Calories 147 Fat 11 g Carbs 9 g Sugar 4 g Protein 5 g Cholesterol 23 mg

Cauliflower Broccoli Mash

Time: 22 minutes

Serve: 3

Ingredients:

- 1 lb cauliflower, cut into florets

- 2 cups broccoli, chopped

- 1 tsp garlic, minced

- 1 tsp dried rosemary

- 1/4 cup olive oil

- Salt

Directions:

1. Add broccoli and cauliflower into the instant pot.

2. Pour enough water into the instant pot to cover broccoli and cauliflower.

3. Seal pot and cook on high pressure for 12 minutes.

4. Once done, allow to release pressure naturally. Remove lid.

5. Drain broccoli and cauliflower and clean the instant pot.

6. Add oil into the instant pot and set the pot on sauté mode.

7. Add broccoli, cauliflower, rosemary, garlic, and salt, and cook for 10 minutes.

8. Mash the broccoli and cauliflower mixture using a masher until smooth.

9. Serve and enjoy.

Nutritional Value (Amount per Serving):

Calories 205 Fat 17 g Carbs 12 g Sugar 5 g Protein 5 g Cholesterol 0 mg

Italian Chicken Soup

Time: 35 minutes

Serve: 6

Ingredients:

- 1 lb chicken breasts, boneless and cut into chunks

- 1 1/2 cups salsa

- 1 tsp Italian seasoning

- 2 tbsp fresh parsley, chopped

- 3 cups chicken stock

- 8 oz cream cheese

- Pepper

- Salt

Directions:

1. Add all ingredients except cream cheese and parsley into the instant pot and stir well.

2. Seal pot and cook on high pressure for 25 minutes.

3. Release pressure using quick release. Remove lid.

4. Remove chicken from pot and shred using a fork.

5. Return shredded chicken to the instant pot.

6. Add cream cheese and stir well and cook on sauté mode until cheese is melted.

7. Serve and enjoy.

Nutritional Value (Amount per Serving):

Calories 300 Fat 19 g Carbs 5 g Sugar 2 g Protein 26 g Cholesterol 109 mg

Tasty Tomatoes Soup

Time: 15 minutes

Serve: 2

Ingredients:

- 14 oz can fire-roasted tomatoes

- 1/2 tsp dried basil

- 1/2 cup heavy cream

- 1/2 cup parmesan cheese, grated

- 1 cup cheddar cheese, grated

- 1 1/2 cups vegetable stock

- 1/4 cup zucchini, grated

- 1/2 tsp dried oregano

- Pepper

- Salt

Directions:

1. Add tomatoes, stock, zucchini, oregano, basil, pepper, and salt into the instant pot and stir well.

2. Seal pot and cook on high pressure for 5 minutes.

3. Release pressure using quick release. Remove lid.

4. Set pot on sauté mode. Add heavy cream, parmesan cheese, and cheddar cheese and stir well and cook until cheese is melted.

5. Serve and enjoy.

Nutritional Value (Amount per Serving):

Calories 460 Fat 35 g Carbs 13 g Sugar 6 g Protein 24 g Cholesterol 117 mg

Cauliflower Spinach Soup

Time: 20 minutes

Serve: 2

Ingredients:

- 3 cups spinach, chopped

- 1 cup cauliflower, chopped

- 2 tbsp olive oil

- 3 cups vegetable broth

- 1/2 cup heavy cream

- 1 tsp garlic powder

- Pepper

- Salt

Directions:

1. Add all ingredients except cream into the instant pot and stir well.

2. Seal pot and cook on high pressure for 10 minutes.

3. Release pressure using quick release. Remove lid.

4. Stir in cream and blend soup using a blender until smooth.

5. Serve and enjoy.

Nutritional Value (Amount per Serving):

Calories 310 Fat 27 g Carbs 7 g Sugar 3 g Protein 10 g Cholesterol 41 mg

Delicious Chicken Salad

Time: 15 minutes

Serve: 4

Ingredients:

- 1 1/2 cups chicken breast, skinless, boneless, and cooked

- 2 tbsp onion, diced

- 1/4 cup olives, diced

- 1/4 cup roasted red peppers, diced

- 1/4 cup cucumbers, diced

- 1/4 cup celery, diced

- 1/4 cup feta cheese, crumbled

- 1/2 tsp onion powder

- 1/2 tbsp fresh lemon juice

- 1 tbsp fresh parsley, chopped

- 1 tbsp fresh dill, chopped

- 2 1/2 tbsp mayonnaise

- 1/4 cup Greek yogurt

- 1/4 tsp pepper

- 1/2 tsp salt

Directions:

1. In a bowl, mix yogurt, onion powder, lemon juice, parsley, dill, mayonnaise, pepper, and salt.

2. Add chicken, onion, olives, red peppers, cucumbers, and feta cheese and stir well.

3. Serve and enjoy.

Nutritional Value (Amount per Serving):

Calories 172 Fat 7.9 g Carbs 6.7 g Sugar 3.1 g Protein 18.1 g Cholesterol 52 mg

Baked Pesto Salmon

Time: 30 minutes

Serve: 5

Ingredients:

- 1 3/4 lbs salmon fillet

- 1/3 cup basil pesto

- 1/4 cup sun-dried tomatoes, drained

- 1/4 cup olives, pitted and chopped

- 1 tbsp fresh dill, chopped

- 1/4 cup capers

- 1/3 cup artichoke hearts

- 1 tsp paprika

- 1/4 tsp salt

Directions:

1. Preheat the oven to 400 F. Cover the pan with parchment paper.
2. Arrange salmon fillet on a prepared baking sheet and season with paprika and salt.
3. Add remaining ingredients on top of salmon and spread evenly.
4. Bake for 20 minutes.
5. Serve and enjoy.

Nutritional Value (Amount per Serving):

Calories 228 Fat 10.7 g Carbs 2.7 g Sugar 0.3 g Protein 31.6 g Cholesterol 70 mg

Easy Shrimp Salad

Time: 15 minutes

Serve: 6

Ingredients:

- 2 lbs shrimp, cooked

- 1/4 cup onion, minced

- 1/4 cup fresh dill, chopped

- 1/3 cup fresh chives, chopped

- 1/2 cup fresh celery, chopped

- 1/4 tsp cayenne pepper

- 1 tbsp fresh lemon juice

- 1 tbsp olive oil

- 1/4 cup mayonnaise

- 1/4 tsp pepper

- 1/4 tsp salt

Directions:

1. In a large bowl, add all ingredients except shrimp and mix well.

2. Add shrimp and toss well.

3. Serve and enjoy.

Nutritional Value (Amount per Serving):

Calories 248 Fat 8.3 g Carbs 6.7 g Sugar 1.1 g Protein 35.2 g Cholesterol 321 mg

Simple Haddock Salad

Time: 15 minutes

Serve: 6

Ingredients:

- 1 lb haddock, cooked

- 1 tbsp green onion, chopped

- 1 tbsp olive oil

- 1 tsp garlic, minced

- Pepper

- Salt

Directions:

1. Cut cooked haddock into bite-size pieces and place on a plate.

2. Season with oil, pepper, and salt

3. Sprinkle garlic and green onion over haddock.

4. Serve and enjoy.

Nutritional Value (Amount per Serving):

Calories 106 Fat 3 g Carbs 0.2 g Sugar 0 g Protein 18.4 g Cholesterol 56 mg

Baked White Fish Fillet

Time: 40 minutes

Serve: 1

Ingredients:

- 8 oz frozen white fish fillet

- 1 tbsp roasted red bell pepper, diced

- 1/2 tsp Italian seasoning

- 1 tbsp fresh parsley, chopped

- 1 1/2 tbsp olive oil

- 1 tbsp lemon juice

Directions:

1. Preheat the oven to 400 F. Line baking sheet with foil.

2. Place a fish fillet on a baking sheet.

3. Drizzle oil and lemon juice over fish. Season with Italian seasoning.

4. Top with roasted bell pepper and parsley and bake for 30 minutes.

5. Serve and enjoy.

Nutritional Value (Amount per Serving):

Calories 383 Fat 22.5 g Carbs 0.8 g Sugar 0.6 g Protein 46.5 g Cholesterol 2 mg

Air Fry Salmon

Time: 25 minutes

Serve: 4

Ingredients:

- 1 lbs salmon, cut into 4 pieces

- 1 tbsp olive oil

- 1/2 tbsp dried rosemary

- 1/4 tsp dried basil

- 1 tbsp dried chives

- Pepper

- Salt

Directions:

1. Place salmon pieces skin side down into the air fryer basket.

2. In a small bowl, mix olive oil, basil, chives, and rosemary.

3. Brush salmon with oil mixture and air fry at 400 F for 15 minutes.

4. Serve and enjoy.

Nutritional Value (Amount per Serving):

Calories 182 Fat 10.6 g Carbs 0.3 g Sugar 0 g Protein 22 g Cholesterol 50 mg

Baked Salmon Patties

Time: 30 minutes

Serve: 4

Ingredients:

- 2 eggs, lightly beaten

- 14 oz can salmon, drained and flaked with a fork

- 1 tbsp garlic, minced

- 1/4 cup almond flour

- 1/2 cup fresh parsley, chopped

- 1 tsp Dijon mustard

- 1/4 tsp pepper

- 1/2 tsp kosher salt

Directions:

1. Preheat the oven to 400 F. Line a baking sheet with parchment paper and set aside.

2. Add all ingredients into the bowl and mix until well combined.

3. Make small patties from the mixture and place on a prepared baking sheet.

4. Bake patties for 10 minutes.

5. Turn patties and bake for 10 minutes more.

6. Serve and enjoy.

Nutritional Value (Amount per Serving):

Calories 216 Fat 11.8 g Carbs 3 g Sugar 0.5 g Protein 24.3 g Cholesterol 136 mg

CPSIA information can be obtained
at www.ICGtesting.com
Printed in the USA
LVHW080709150321
681563LV00017B/546

9 781801 456746